sizzling
barbecue

www.myownbbq.com
www.vermontcastings.com

sizzling
barbecue

Published by:
TRIDENT PRESS INTERNATIONAL
801 12th Avenue South, Suite 400
Naples, Fl 34102 USA
Tel: + 1 239 649 7077
Email: tridentpress@worldnet.att.net
Websites: www.trident-international.com

Sizzling Barbecue
© Trident Press International

Publisher
Simon St. John Bailey

Editor-in-chief
Isabel Toyos

Design and Lay Out
Eleanor Loiterstein

Food Editor
A. Giribaldi

Includes Index
ISBN 1582796718
UPC 6 15269 96718 8

2006 Edition
Printed in The United States of America

introduction

You don't have to envy the grill next door
when you've got your own hot ticket to the
country's most popular pastime. And, once
you fall in love with one of the gorgeous grills
from Vermont Castings, you can make
out-of-doors cooking a year 'round affair.
Hope you enjoy this compilation
of sumptuous barbecue recipes!

Note: Some recipes in this book are intended
for 'general grilling', therefore results may vary.

Direct & Indirect Cooking Methods on Gas Barbecue Grills

One of the keys to extending your range of grilling capabilities is a fundamental understanding of the two common methods of cooking, **Direct** and **Indirect** cooking.

In the **Direct cooking method**, food is placed directly above the heat source. This method is used in searing for example where you require high and immediate heat to quickly brown the outside layer of meats thereby sealing in their juices to enhance flavor. On the grill this is accomplished using one or both of your main burners and placing the food on the porcelain cooking grids directly over the burners. This may be done with the grill hood either open or closed.

In the **Indirect cooking method**, food is placed on the grill offset from the heat source. With the grill lid closed reflected heat surrounds the food cooking it more evenly and gently. This approximates the action of a convection oven where heat is circulated by the use of a fan to achieve a similar result. This method is perfect for cooking roasts of any kind but is also useful whenever you want to slow cook or bake a wide variety of foods. Indirect cooking on your grill is accomplished using one of the main burners and placing the food on the porcelain cooking grid above the opposite burner, or on the warming rack burner. The grill hood should always be closed when employing the indirect cooking method.

Basic Barbecue Sauces

Barbecue Sauce

1 tablespoon vegetable oil; 1 onion, chopped; 1 clove garlic, crushed; 1 teaspoon mustard powder; 1 tablespoon Worcestershire sauce; 1 tablespoon brown sugar; 3 tablespoons tomato sauce; 1 teaspoon chili sauce; 3/4 cup/185 ml/6 fl oz beef stock; freshly ground black pepper.

Heat oil in a saucepan and cook onion and garlic for 3-4 minutes or until soft. Stir in mustard powder, Worcestershire sauce, sugar, tomato sauce, chili sauce and stock. Bring to the boil, then reduce heat and simmer for 8-10 minutes or until sauce reduces and thickens slightly. Season to taste with black pepper.

Makes 1 cup/250 ml/8 fl oz

Sweet and Sour Barbecue Sauce

1 tablespoon vegetable oil; 1 small onion, chopped; 1 red pepper, chopped; 1 tablespoon soy sauce; 2 tablespoons honey; 1 tablespoon tomato paste (purée); 2 tablespoons cornflour; 1/2 cup/125 ml/4 fl oz cider vinegar; 1/2 cup/125 ml/4 fl oz chicken stock or water; 440 g/14 oz canned pineapple pieces, drained.

1. Heat oil in a saucepan and cook onion and red pepper for 4-5 minutes or until soft. Place soy sauce, honey, tomato paste (purée), cornflour and vinegar in a bowl and mix to combine.
2. Stir cornflour mixture into vegetables, then stir in stock or water. Cook, stirring, over a medium heat for 2-3 minutes or until sauce boils and thickens. Stir in pineapple pieces and cook for 2-3 minutes longer.

Makes 2 cups/500 ml/16 fl oz

Difficulty scale

■□□I Easy to do

■■□I Requires attention

■■■I Requires experience

onion
and parmesan breads

■ ■ □ I Cooking time: 10 minutes - Preparation time: 2 hours 15 minutes

ingredients

> **2 teaspoons active dry yeast**
> **2¹/₂ cups/600 ml/1 pt warm water**
> **5¹/₂ cups/700 g/1 lb 7 oz flour**
> **4 spring onions, chopped**
> **4 tablespoons finely grated Parmesan cheese**
> **2 teaspoons sea salt**
> **1 tablespoon poppy seeds**

method

1. Place yeast and water in a bowl and mix to dissolve. Stand in a warm draught-free place for 5 minutes or until foamy.
2. Combine flour, spring onions, Parmesan cheese and salt in a bowl. Stir in yeast mixture (a) and continue mixing to make a smooth dough. Turn dough onto a lightly floured surface and knead for about 10 minutes or until smooth and elastic.
3. Place dough in a lightly oiled bowl and roll around bowl to coat surface with oil. Cover bowl and place in a warm draught-free place for 2 hours or until doubled in size.
4. Preheat barbecue to a medium heat. Knock dough down and knead lightly. Divide into 8 pieces. Roll out each piece on a lightly floured surface to form a round about 5 mm/¹/₄ in thick (b).
5. Pierce dough rounds all over (c), then lightly brush with oil and sprinkle with poppy seeds.
6. Place bread on barbecue grill and cook for 3-4 minutes each side. Serve warm.

....
Makes 8

tip from the chef

To make a delicious spread for these breads, process or blend 250 g/8 oz ricotta cheese until smooth. Stir in 2 tablespoons chopped fresh chives and 2 teaspoons crushed black peppercorns.

a

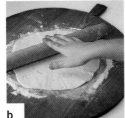

b

c

sage and pancetta pizzas

■□□ | Cooking time: 10 minutes - Preparation time: 15 minutes

method

1. Preheat barbecue to a high heat. Divide pizza dough into 4 portions and roll into rounds about 1 cm/1/2 in thick. Lightly brush dough rounds with oil, place on barbecue grill and cook for 3-5 minutes or until well browned and crisp.

2. Flip pizza bases. Top cooked side with overlapping slices of tomatoes, pancetta and cheese. Scatter with sage leaves and black pepper to taste. Cook for 3-5 minutes longer or until base is golden and crisp and topping warm. Serve immediately.

....
Makes 4

ingredients

> **1 quantity pizza dough**

sage and pancetta topping
> **2 tomatoes, thinly sliced**
> **250 g/8 oz pancetta, thinly sliced**
> **250 g/8 oz bocconcini cheese, sliced**
> **2 tablespoons fresh sage leaves**
> **freshly ground black pepper**

tip from the chef

To make pizza dough, place 1 teaspoon active dry yeast, pinch sugar and 2/3 cup/170 ml/ 5 1/2 fl oz warm water in a bowl and mix to dissolve. Stand for 5 minutes or until foamy. Place 2 cups/250 g/8 oz flour and 1/2 teaspoon salt in a food processor and pulse once or twice to sift. With machine running, slowly pour in yeast mixture and 1/4 cup/ 60 ml/2 fl oz olive oil and process to form a rough dough. Knead dough until soft and shiny. Place dough in an oiled bowl, cover with plastic food wrap and place in a warm draught-free place for 1-1 1/2 hours or until doubled in size. Knock down and knead lightly.

chicken
and basil pizzas

■□□ | Cooking time: 15 minutes - Preparation time: 15 minutes

ingredients

> **1 quantity pizza dough (page 8)**

chicken and basil topping

> **8 plum (egg or Italian) tomatoes, thickly sliced**
> **2 boneless chicken breast fillets, cut into thick slices**
> **2 tablespoons olive oil**
> **freshly ground black pepper**
> **75 g/2¹/2 oz marinated olives, pitted**
> **¹/2 bunch fresh basil, shredded**
> **25 g/4 oz grated Parmesan cheese**

method

1. Preheat barbecue to a high heat. Lightly brush tomato and chicken slices with oil and season with black pepper to taste. Place on barbecue and cook for 2 minutes each side or until chicken is brown and cooked through.

2. Divide pizza dough into 8 portions and roll into rounds about 1 cm/1/2 in thick (a). Lightly brush dough with oil, place on barbecue grill and cook for 3-4 minutes or until golden and crisp on one side (b).

3. Flip pizza bases. Top cooked side with tomatoes and chicken, then scatter with olives and basil and sprinkle with Parmesan cheese. Cook for 3-5 minutes longer or until base is golden and crisp and topping warm (c). Serve immediately.

Makes 8

tip from the chef

Kneading is an important technique when making pizza dough. Kneading by hand will take about 5-10 minutes and the dough should be elastic, soft and shiny. Knocking after the first rising of the dough, knocks out the air bubbles which have developed during rising and ensures a good textured cooked product. **a**

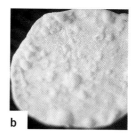

b

c

char-grilled
vegetables

■□□ | Cooking time: 15 minutes - Preparation time: 10 minutes

method

1. Preheat barbecue to a high heat. Carefully pull back husks from sweet corn cobs, keeping them attached, and remove silk. Tie a string around the husks to form a handle. Cook sweet corn cobs in boiling water in a saucepan for 2-3 minutes or until kernels soften slightly. Drain.

2. Brush sweet corn cobs with oil. Place asparagus, zucchini, leeks, tomatoes and black pepper to taste in a bowl. Drizzle with oil and toss to coat.

3. Place all the vegetables on barbecue grill and cook, turning several times, until well browned and tender. Serve with lemon wedges.

ingredients

> **2 cobs sweet corn with husks**
> **1-2 tablespoons chili or herb oil**
> **185 g/6 oz asparagus spears**
> **2 zucchini, halved lengthwise**
> **4 baby leeks**
> **4 plum (egg or Italian) tomatoes, halved**
> **freshly ground black pepper**
> **lemon wedges**

Serves 6

tip from the chef
Watch a lit barbecue at all times and keep children and pets away from hot barbecues and equipment.

char-grilled
mushrooms and toast

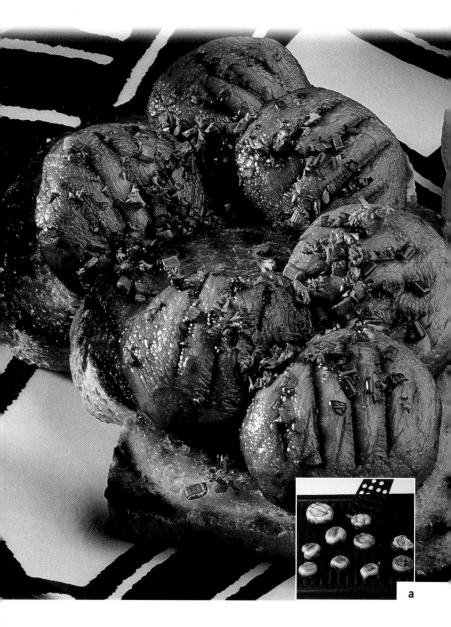

a

■☐☐ | Cooking time: 10 minutes - Preparation time: 10 minutes

method

1. Preheat barbecue to a medium heat. Brush mushrooms with oil and cook on lightly oiled barbecue (a) for 4-5 minutes or until cooked.
2. Brush both sides of the bread with remaining oil and cook for 2-3 minutes each side (b) or until golden.
3. Rub one side of each bread slice with cut side of garlic clove (c). Top each slice with mushrooms, sprinkle with parsley, chives and basil. Season to taste with black pepper (d) and serve immediately.

Serves 2

ingredients

> 6 flat mushrooms
> 1/4 cup/60 ml/2 fl oz olive oil
> 2 thick slices of bread
> 1 clove garlic, cut in half
> 2 teaspoons finely chopped fresh parsley
> 2 teaspoons snipped fresh chives
> 1 teaspoon finely chopped fresh basil
> freshly ground black pepper

tip from the chef
This delicious first course takes only minutes to cook.

 b
 c
 d

rösti with gravlax

■□□ | Cooking time: 10 minutes - Preparation time: 10 minutes

ingredients

> ¹/2 cup/125 g/4 oz sour cream
> 250 g/8 oz salmon gravlax
> lemon wedges

vegetable rösti

> 3 large potatoes, grated
> 2 zucchini, grated
> 2 carrots, grated
> 1 leek, shredded
> ¹/2 cup/60 g/2 oz flour
> 3 tablespoons finely grated Parmesan cheese
> 1 tablespoon chopped fresh mint
> 1 tablespoon Dijon mustard
> 4 eggs, lightly beaten
> freshly ground black pepper

method

1. Preheat barbecue to a medium heat. To make rösti, place potatoes, zucchini, carrots, leek, flour, Parmesan cheese, mint, mustard, eggs and black pepper to taste in a bowl and mix to combine.

2. Place large spoonfuls of vegetable mixture on oiled barbecue plate, press with a spatula to flatten and cook for 5 minutes each side or until golden and crisp. Remove rösti from barbecue and keep warm. Repeat with remaining mixture.

3. To serve, place one or two rösti on each serving plate, top with a spoonful of sour cream, some salmon gravlax and black pepper to taste. Serve with lemon wedges.

··········
Serves 6

tip from the chef

You will need about 440 g/14 oz potatoes for the rösti. For a cocktail party make tiny rösti and serve this tempting starter as finger food.

fish burgers with aïoli

■ ■ ☐ I Cooking time: 10 minutes - Preparation time: 20 minutes

method

1. Preheat barbecue to a medium heat.
2. To make aïoli, place garlic, mustard, egg yolks and vinegar in a food processor or blender and process to combine. With machine running, slowly add olive oil in a thin stream and continue processing until mixture is thick and creamy. If mixture is too thick, add a little warm water to thin it.
3. To make marinade, place chervil or parsley, lime juice, oil and black peppercorns to taste in a shallow dish and mix to combine. Add fish, turn to coat and marinate for 5 minutes.
4. Drain fish and cook on oiled barbecue grill for 1-2 minutes each side or until flesh flakes when tested with a fork.
5. To assemble, toast buns on barbecue grill until golden. Top base of each bun with some lettuce leaves, a fish fillet and a spoonful of aïoli, then cover with top of bun.

ingredients

> 4 fillets blue-eye cod or other firm white fish
> 4 wholemeal buns, split
> 125 g/4 oz assorted lettuce leaves

aïoli

> 2 cloves garlic, crushed
> 2 teaspoons Dijon mustard
> 3 egg yolks
> 1 tablespoon white vinegar
> 1 cup/250 ml/8 fl oz olive oil

pepper and herb marinade

> 2 tablespoons chopped fresh chervil or parsley
> 2 tablespoons lime juice
> 1 tablespoon olive oil
> crushed black peppercorns

....
Makes 4 burgers

tip from the chef

As a side dish for these burgers, toss boiled potato wedges with paprika, cumin, black pepper and oil, cook on barbecue until crisp and sprinkle with sea salt.

smoked
salmon fillet

■□□ I Cooking time: 10 minutes - Preparation time: 20 minutes

ingredients

> 125 g/4 oz hickory smoking chips
> 1 1/2 cups/375 ml/12 fl oz dry white wine
> 1 kg/2 lb fillet salmon, skinned and visible bones removed
> 1 tablespoon vegetable oil
> 2 limes, each cut into 8 thin slices
> 16 fresh dill sprigs
> crushed black peppercorns
> toasted bagel

method

1. Preheat covered barbecue to a medium-low heat. Place smoking chips and wine in a non-reactive metal dish and soak for 20 minutes. Place dish containing smoking chips in barbecue over hot coals, cover barbecue with lid and heat for 5 minutes or until liquid is hot.
2. Cut salmon into 8 equal pieces (a) and brush with oil. Place 2 lime slices and 2 dill sprigs on each piece of salmon (b), then sprinkle with black peppercorns to taste.
3. Place salmon on oiled barbecue grill, cover barbecue with lid and smoke for 5 minutes (c). You may wish to intensify the smoke flavor by extending the cooking time according to your taste. Serve salmon on slices of toasted bagel, with Béarnaise sauce if desired.

....

Serves 8

tip from the chef

When using wood or wood products for barbecuing or smoking, always use untreated wood. Those products specifically sold for barbecuing and smoking will be free of chemicals. Hickory wood is a popular choice for smoking, but there are other woods available which impart different flavors –so experiment and find your favorite.

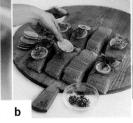

a

b

c

herb-infused fish

■□□ | Cooking time: 20 minutes - Preparation time: 15 minutes

method

1. Preheat barbecue to a high heat. Line one side of a large hinged fish rack with some thyme, rosemary and half the lemon slices (a).
2. Place garlic and black peppercorns in cavity of fish (b). Brush fish generously with oil and place on herbs in rack. Top with remaining lemon slices and some more rosemary and thyme. Close rack (c).
3. Place fish on barbecue and cook for 8-10 minutes each side or until flesh flakes when tested with a fork.

Serves 6

ingredients

> 2 bunches fresh lemon thyme sprigs
> 1 bunch fresh rosemary sprigs
> 2 lemons, sliced
> 3 cloves garlic, peeled
> 6 black peppercorns
> 1.5 kg/3 lb whole fish such as bream, sea perch or snapper, cleaned
> 2 tablespoons olive oil

tip from the chef

Hinged wire racks are a useful accessory for the barbecue cook and are available in many sizes and shapes. The one used in this recipe is designed for cooking whole fish, other shapes include square or rectangular ones which are suitable for cooking burgers and fish fillets and cutlets, or any delicate food which threatens to fall apart when you try to turn it over. To prevent sticking, always oil the rack well before placing the food on it.

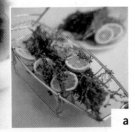
a

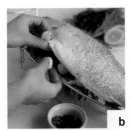
b

c

oysters
and mussels in shells

■□□ | Cooking time: 10 minutes - Preparation time: 5 minutes

method

1. Preheat barbecue to a high heat. Place mussels and oysters on barbecue grill and cook for 3-5 minutes or until mussel shells open and oysters are warm. Discard any mussels that do not open after 5 minutes cooking.

2. Place butter, parsley, lemon juice, orange juice and wine in a heavy-based saucepan, place on barbecue and cook, stirring, for 2 minutes or until mixture is bubbling. Place mussels and oysters on a serving platter, drizzle with butter mixture and serve immediately.

ingredients

> 500 g/1 lb mussels, scrubbed and beards removed
> 24 oysters in half shells
> 60 g/2 oz butter, softened
> 1 tablespoon chopped fresh parsley
> 2 tablespoons lemon juice
> 1 tablespoon orange juice
> 1 tablespoon white wine

....

Serves 6

tip from the chef

Mussels will live out of water for up to 7 days if treated correctly. To keep mussels alive, place them in a bucket, cover with a wet towel and top with ice. Store in a cool place and as the ice melts, drain off the water and replace ice. It is important that the mussels do not sit in the water or they will drown.

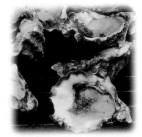

spiced
chicken sandwiches

■ ■ □ | Cooking time: 10 minutes - Preparation time: 20 minutes

method

1. Preheat barbecue to a medium heat.
2. To make marinade, place yogurt, coriander, curry paste, chutney and lemon juice in a shallow dish and mix to combine. Add chicken breasts, turn to coat and marinate for 20 minutes.
3. To make raita, cut cucumber in half, lengthwise and scrape out seeds. Cut cucumber into fine slices and place in a bowl. Add yogurt, garlic and lemon juice and mix to combine. Cover and chill until ready to serve.
4. Drain chicken and cook on oiled barbecue grill for 4 minutes each side or until tender and cooked through. To serve, place chicken fillets on 4 pieces of bread, then top with tomatoes and raita and remaining pieces of bread.

Makes 4 sandwiches

ingredients

> 4 boneless chicken breast fillets
> 4 pieces Turkish (pide) bread, halved
> 4 tomatoes, sliced

spiced yogurt marinade

> 1/2 cup/100 g/3 1/2 oz natural yogurt
> 4 tablespoons chopped fresh coriander
> 2 tablespoons mild red curry paste
> 2 tablespoons mango chutney
> 2 tablespoons lemon juice

cucumber raita

> 1 cucumber
> 1 cup/200 g/6 1/2 oz thick natural yogurt
> 1 clove garlic, crushed
> 1 tablespoon lemon juice

tip from the chef

Turkish bread (pide) is a flat white leavened bread similar to Italian flatbread. It is usually baked in ovals measuring 30-40 cm/12-16 in. If Turkish bread is unavailable, country-style Italian bread, rye bread, sour dough, ciabatta or focaccia are all good alternatives for this recipe.

quick
chicken satay

Cooking time: 35 minutes - Preparation time: 15minutes

method

1. Place oil, soy sauce, garlic and ginger in a bowl and mix to combine. Add chicken and marinate for 15 minutes.
2. Drain chicken, thread onto lightly oiled skewers and cook on a preheated medium barbecue for 15-20 minutes or until chicken is cooked.
3. To make sauce, heat oil in a saucepan over a medium heat, add garlic and ginger and cook, stirring, for 2 minutes. Stir in stock, coconut milk and soy sauce, bring to simmering and simmer for 5 minutes.
4. Add peanut butter and simmer for 5 minutes longer. Just prior to serving, stir in chili sauce. Serve sauce with chicken.

Serves 4

ingredients

> 1 tablespoon vegetable oil
> 1 tablespoon soy sauce
> 1 large clove garlic, crushed
> 1/2 teaspoon finely grated fresh ginger
> 500 g/1 lb boneless chicken thigh or breast fillets, skinned and cut into 2.5 cm/1 in cubes

satay sauce
> 1 teaspoon vegetable oil
> 2 large cloves garlic, crushed
> 2 teaspoons finely grated fresh ginger
> 1 cup/250 ml/8 fl oz chicken stock
> 1 cup/250 ml/8 fl oz coconut milk
> 1 tablespoon soy sauce
> 2 tablespoons crunchy peanut butter
> 2 teaspoons sweet chili sauce

tip from the chef
The sauce can be made in advance and stored in a sealed container in the refrigerator for 5-7 days. Reheat over a low heat before serving. If sweet chili sauce is not available mix ordinary chili sauce with a little brown sugar.

pakistani
chicken skewers

■□□ | Cooking time: 10 minutes - Preparation time: 10 minutes

ingredients

> **1 onion, chopped**
> **2 cloves garlic, crushed**
> **1 tablespoon finely grated fresh ginger**
> **1 tablespoon mild masala paste**
> **1/2 cup/100 g/31/2 oz natural yogurt**
> **8 boneless chicken breast fillets, cut into 2 cm/ 3/4 in cubes**

method

1. Place onion, garlic, ginger, masala paste and yogurt into food processor or blender and process until smooth.
2. Transfer yogurt mixture to a bowl, add chicken and toss to coat. Cover and marinate for 2 hours.
3. Thread chicken onto lightly oiled skewers and cook on a lightly oiled preheated hot barbecue for 10 minutes or until chicken is tender.

....
Serves 6-8

tip from the chef

When using bamboo skewers, soak them in cold water for at least an hour before using them on a barbecue; this will prevent them from burning. Lightly oiling the skewers ensures that the food does not stick to them during cooking.

oriental
chicken kebabs

GRILLING TIPS

A few helpful hints will ensure that your grilling results are perfect every time.

- Apply a light coating of cooking oil to your cooking grids before grilling, to prevent foods from sticking.
- Cook similar portion sizes together, so that they all cook evenly.
- Use tongs to turn foods on the Grill.
- Never pierce foods while they are cooking on the Grill, as this will dry them out.
- On foods such as pork chops and steak, slit the fat strip to prevent the meat from curling during cooking.
- Turn foods infrequently. Some chefs say that a good steak should never be turned more than once.
- Apply sugar-based sauces such as commercial barbecue sauces only during the latter stages of cooking, to prevent charring.
- Soak the string you use to tie up roasts and poultry on the Rotisserie spit to protect it from burning. Also, soak the wooden skewers that you intend to use for kebabs for several minutes before using them for cooking.
- Use a disposable aluminum tray filled with water, fruit juice, wine or a marinade to add extra flavor and moisture to slow-cooked foods like roasts, whole chickens, turkeys or ducks. Place the tray on top of the sear plates below the Grill surface and immediately under the foods being cooked. This will buffer the heat from below, thereby slowing the cooking process and protecting the bottom of the food from overcooking.
- Check the tray periodically during cooking and keep it filled with liquid.

WARNING: Never let the tray boil dry. That could be hazardous, as grease from fatty foods that have collected in the tray could ignite and possibly cause bodily injury or property damage.

NOTE: Always trim excess fat from your foods to reduce the occurrence of flare-ups during cooking.

BRING OUT THE BEST IN YOUR FOOD AND YOU

COMPLIMENTS o
VERMONT CASTINGS SIGNA

Type of Food	Weight/ Thickness	Cooking Temperature	Cooking Time
Beef			
Burgers	1 inch	400-450° F.	Rare: 4-7min. Medium: 7-10 min. Well Done:10-12 min.
Roasts			
Blade, Sirloin Tip		350°	Rare: 18-20min./lb. Medium: 20-25 min./lb. Well Done: 25-30 min./lb.
Steaks			
Porterhouse, Rib, Ribeye, Sirloin, T-Bone	1 inch	Max. (To sear) 400-450° F. (To finish)	Rare: 4-7min. Medium: 7-10 min. Well Done: 10-12 min.
Filet Mignon	2 inches	Max. (To sear) 400-450° F. (To finish)	Rare: 15-17 min. Medium: 17-19 min. Well Done: 19-22 min.
Poultry			
Chicken, Parts		325 –350° F.	30-45 min.
Chicken, Whole	3 –4 lbs.	325 –350° F.	20 min./lb.
Chicken Breasts,	1-2 lbs.	325 –350° F.	12-15 min.
Boneless			
Cornish Hens	1–1-1/2 lbs.	325 –350° F.	45-60 min.
Duck	4 –5 lbs.	325 –350° F.	18-20 min./lb.
Turkey	13 –25 lbs.	325 –350° F.	20 min./lb.
Fish & Seafood			
Fish			
Fillets	1-1-1/2 inch	400-450° F.	10-15 min.
Steaks	1 -2 lbs.	325-350° F.	20-30 min.
Whole Fish	2 -4 lbs.	325-350° F.	30-50 min.
Seafood			
Lobster	1-1/2-2 lbs.	400-450° F.	15 min.
Shrimp	Large	325-350° F.	5-6 min.

BRING OUT THE BEST

RE SERIES GRILLS

Type of Food	Weight/ Thickness	Cooking Temperature	Cooking Time
Pork			
Chops	1 inch	400-450° F.	25-30 min.
Ham			
Steak	1 inch	400-450° F.	12-15 min.
Whole ham	12-14 lbs. Bone in	325 –350° F.	Medium: 20-25 min./lb. Well Done: 25-30min./lb.
	4-5 lbs. Boneless	325 –350° F.	50-60 min.
Ribs			
Back, Side	5-6 lbs.	325-350° F.	Medium: 25-27 min./lb. Well Done: 27-30 min./lb.
Roasts			
Butt, Loin, Shoulder	3-5lbs.	325-350° F.	1-1-1/2 hrs.
Tenderloin		375-400° F.	Medium: 30-35 min./lb. Well Done: 35-40 min./lb.
Sausage			12-20 min.
Lamb			
Chops			
Loin, Rib, Shoulder	1 inch	400-450° F.	Rare: 7-9 min Medium: 10-13 min. Well Done: 14-17 min.
Roast			
Crown Roast	2-4 lbs.	325-350° F.	40-45 min./lb.
Leg	5-9 lbs.	325-350° F.	30-35 min./lb.

YOUR FOOD AND YOU.

COOKING TIME CHART

Type of Food	Cooking Temperature	Cooking Time	Cooking Time
Vegetables			
Asparagus	325-350° F.	6-8 min.	Cut off ends of stems. Lay across the grills.
Beans	325-350° F.	30-35 min.	Wrap in foil with butter or margarine. Turn over once.
Carrots	325-350° F.	20-30 min.	Cook directly on the grill.
Corn on the Cob	325-350° F.	25-35 min.	Soak in cold water for 15 minutes. Cook with husk on.
Eggplant	325-350° F.	6-8 min./side	Cut into slices and coat with oil.
Mushrooms	325-350° F.	6-8 min.	Cook directly on the grill.
Onions	325-350° F.	40-45 min.	Wrap in foil Turn over once during cooking.
Peppers	400-450° F.	15-20 min.	Remove charred skin before eating.
Potatoes	325-350° F.	50-60 min.	Wrap in foil.Turn over once.
Roasted Garlic	325-350° F.	30-40 min.	Cut off top of bud and lightly coat with Olive oil. Wrap in foil.
Tomatoes	325-350° F.	5-7 min.	Cut in half and coat in Olive oil.
Zucchini	325-350° F.	6-8 min./side	Cut into slices and coat with oil.

BRING OUT THE BEST IN YOUR FOOD AND YOU

■□□ I Cooking time: 10 minutes - Preparation time: 20 minutes

method

1. Preheat barbecue to a high heat.
2. To make marinade, place sugar, lime leaves, if using, chili, soy sauce and lime juice in a bowl and mix to combine. Add chicken, toss to coat and marinate for 20 minutes. Drain chicken.
3. Thread chicken and mushrooms onto lightly oiled skewers and cook on oiled barbecue grill, turning and basting with reserved marinade, for 5 minutes or until chicken is tender and cooked.
4. Place snow pea sprouts or watercress, carrots and spring onions in a bowl. Combine sugar and lime juice, pour over salad and toss. Pile salad onto serving plates, then top with chicken kebabs.

ingredients

> 3 boneless chicken breast fillets, sliced
> 12 shiitake mushrooms
> 185 g/6 oz snow pea sprouts or watercress
> 2 carrots, shredded
> 4 spring onions, chopped
> 2 teaspoons sugar
> 2 tablespoons lime juice

chili and lime marinade

> 1 tablespoon brown sugar
> 3 kaffir lime leaves, shredded (optional)
> 1 fresh red chili, chopped
> 2 tablespoons soy sauce
> 1 tablespoon lime juice

Serves 6

tip from the chef

Try kebabs with barbecued garlic flatbread. To make it, combine 1 tablespoon olive oil and 2 cloves garlic, crushed, and lightly brush both sides of 3 pieces lavash bread or pitta bread rounds. Cook on barbecue grill for about 1-2 minutes each side or until golden. Break into pieces to serve.

greek
honey lemon chicken

■□□ I Cooking time: 20 minutes - Preparation time: 10 minutes

method

1. To make marinade, place garlic, rosemary, oregano, oil, lemon juice and honey in a ceramic or glass dish and mix to combine. Add chicken, cover and marinate at room temperature for 15 minutes.

2. Drain chicken and reserve marinade. Cook chicken, basting frequently with reserved marinade, on a preheated medium barbecue for 10 minutes each side or until cooked. Place any remaining marinade in a saucepan and heat over a low heat. Serve with chicken.

Serves 4

ingredients

> 8 boneless chicken thigh fillets or 4 boneless chicken breast fillets, skinned and all visible fat removed

lemon honey marinade

> 5 cloves garlic, crushed
> 2 teaspoons dried rosemary
> 1 teaspoon dried oregano
> 1/4 cup/60 ml/2 fl oz olive oil
> 1/4 cup/60 ml/2 fl oz lemon juice
> 1 tablespoon honey

tip from the chef

For a more pronounced flavor marinate chicken in the refrigerator overnight.

lemon
spit-roasted chickens

■■□ | Cooking time: 1 hour - Preparation time 15 minutes

ingredients

> **2 x 1.2 kg/2¹/₂ lb chickens**
> **1 lemon, quartered**
> **2 onions, quartered**
> **4 sprigs fresh rosemary**
> **4 cloves garlic, halved**

herb butter

> **125 g/4 oz butter, softened**
> **2 tablespoons chopped fresh rosemary**
> **2 tablespoons chopped fresh lemon thyme**

method

1. Preheat barbecue to a high heat. Wash chickens and pat dry with absorbent kitchen paper. Place 2 lemon quarters, 4 onion quarters, 2 rosemary sprigs and 4 garlic clove halves in the cavity of each chicken (a).

2. To make herb butter, place butter, chopped rosemary and thyme in a bowl and mix to combine. Using your fingers, carefully loosen the skin over the breasts of the chickens, then spread butter under it (b).

3. Thread chickens onto the rotisserie spit and secure with clamps at both ends (c) to stop chickens from spinning when cooking. Place rotisserie spit over barbecue and cook for 1 hour or until chickens are tender.

....
Serves 6-8

tip from the chef

Spit-roasting is best done on a gas barbecue with volcanic rock or charcoal. To prevent flare-ups during cooking place a tray of water in the barbecue under the chickens. This catches the fat which drips out during cooking. Check the manufacturer's instructions on how to install the rotisserie spit on your barbecue.

a

b

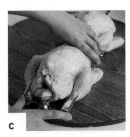

c

festive
smoked turkey

■■☐ I Cooking time: 3-3¹/₄ hours - Preparation time 10 minutes

ingredients
> **1 cup/125 g/4 oz smoking chips**
> **¹/2 cup/125 ml/4 fl oz brandy**
> **3 kg/6 lb turkey, neck and giblets removed, trimmed of excess fat**
> **¹/2 cup/125 ml/4 fl oz chicken stock**
> **2 tablespoons vegetable oil**

sage and rice stuffing
> **60 g/2 oz butter**
> **1 leek, thinly sliced**
> **4 spring onions, chopped**
> **3 strips bacon, chopped**
> **1 cup/60 g/2 oz breadcrumbs, made from stale bread**
> **60 g/2 oz pecans, chopped**
> **2 tablespoons chopped fresh sage or 1 teaspoon dried sage**
> **1¹/2 cups/280 g/9 oz rice, cooked**

method
1. Soak smoking chips in brandy in a non-reactive metal dish for one hour.
2. To make stuffing, melt butter in a frying pan over a medium heat, add leek and spring onions and cook, stirring, for 3 minutes. Add bacon and cook for 5 minutes longer. Add breadcrumbs, pecans and sage and cook, stirring, for 5 minutes or until breadcrumbs are crisp. Remove from heat, add rice and mix to combine.
3. Preheat covered barbecue to a medium heat. Place dish, with smoking chips in, on barbecue grill, cover barbecue with lid and heat for 5-10 minutes or until liquid is hot.
4. Spoon stuffing into body cavity of turkey. Secure openings with metal or bamboo skewers. Tuck wings under body and tie legs together. Thread turkey onto the rotisserie spit and tie it up with string, previously soaked. Combine stock and oil and brush over turkey.
5. Place rotisserie spit over barbecue, cover barbecue with lid and smoke, basting turkey frequently and adding brandy to dish if necessary, for 2¹/2-3 hours or until turkey is cooked.

....
Serves 6-8

italian hamburgers

a

b

■□□ | Cooking time: 8 minutes - Preparation time: 15 minutes

method

1. To make patties, place beef, sun-dried tomatoes, parsley, basil, garlic and Worcestershire sauce in a bowl and mix to combine (a). Shape mixture into 8 mini patties (b), place on a plate lined with plastic food wrap and chill until required.

2. Preheat barbecue to a high heat. Brush eggplant slices and pepper quarters with oil (c) and cook on barbecue grill for 2 minutes each side or until tender. Place in a bowl, add vinegar and toss to combine.

3. Reduce barbecue heat to medium, then cook patties for 4 minutes each side (d) or until cooked to your liking. To assemble, spread base of rolls with pesto, then top with some rocket leaves, a patty, some slices of eggplant and a piece of red pepper and cover with top of roll. Serve immediately.

Makes 8 mini hamburgers

ingredients

> 2 small eggplant, thinly sliced
> 2 red peppers, quartered
> 2 tablespoons olive oil
> 1/3 cup/90 ml/3 fl oz balsamic vinegar
> 8 mini rosetta rolls, split
> 3 tablespoons ready-made pesto
> 125 g/4 oz rocket leaves

beef patties

> 500 g/1 lb lean beef mince
> 3 tablespoons finely chopped sun-dried tomatoes
> 2 tablespoons chopped fresh parsley
> 1 tablespoon chopped fresh basil
> 2 cloves garlic, crushed
> 1 tablespoon Worcestershire sauce

c

d

tip from the chef
Mini hamburgers are a creative alternative for a teenagers' barbecue.

oriental
pork ribs

■□□ | Cooking time: 1 hour 50 minutes - Preparation time: 20 minutes

ingredients

> 1.5 kg/3 lb pork spareribs
> 2 cloves garlic, crushed
> 1 tablespoon finely grated fresh ginger
> 1 tablespoon chopped fresh coriander
> 1 teaspoon five spice powder
> 1/4 cup/60 ml/2 fl oz soy sauce
> 2 tablespoons sweet chili sauce
> 2 tablespoons hoisin sauce
> 1 tablespoon tomato sauce
> 1 tablespoon sherry
> 1 teaspoon rice vinegar

method

1. Place ribs on a wire rack set in a baking dish and bake at 180°C/350°F/Gas 4 for 1 1/2 hours. Set aside to cool slightly.
2. Preheat barbecue to a medium heat. Place garlic, ginger, coriander, five spice powder, soy sauce, chili sauce, hoisin sauce, tomato sauce, sherry and vinegar in a bowl and mix to combine. Add ribs and toss to coat.
3. Drain ribs and reserve liquid. Place ribs on lightly oiled barbecue plate and cook, turning and basting frequently with reserved liquid, for 10 minutes or until ribs are tender.

....
Serves 6

tip from the chef

Five spice powder is a pungent, fragrant, spicy and slightly sweet powder which is a mixture of star anise, fennel, Szechwan peppercorns, cloves and cinnamon. It adds a delicate anise flavor to foods.

chili peanut ribs

■□□ | Cooking time: 10 minutes - Preparation time: 5 minutes

method

1. Place oil, garlic, ginger, chilies, curry paste and coconut milk in a bowl and mix to combine.
2. Place ribs in shallow glass or ceramic dish, pour over coconut milk mixture, turn to coat, cover and set aside to marinate for 2 hours.
3. Drain ribs and cook on a lightly oiled preheated hot barbecue for 5 minutes each side or until meat is tender.

Serves 4

ingredients

> 1 tablespoon vegetable oil
> 2 cloves garlic, crushed
> 2 tablespoons finely grated fresh ginger
> 3 small fresh red chilies, finely chopped
> 3 tablespoons satay curry paste
> 1 cup/250 ml/8 fl oz coconut milk
> 1 kg/2 lb beef spare ribs

tip from the chef

To store fresh ginger, peel and place in a glass jar. Cover with sherry or green ginger wine, store in the refrigerator and use as you would fresh ginger. Ginger will keep in this way for many months. The sherry or wine left after the ginger was used is ideal either for cooking or dressings.

herbed
and spiced pork loin

■■□ | Cooking time: 2 hours 30 minutes - Preparation time: 20 minutes

ingredients

> **2 kg/4 lb boneless pork loin, rolled and rind scored at 2 cm/3/4 in intervals**

herb and spice marinade
> **1 onion, chopped**
> **2 tablespoons crushed pink peppercorns**
> **2 tablespoons crushed green peppercorns**
> **2 tablespoons ground coriander**
> **1 tablespoon freshly ground black pepper**
> **1 tablespoon ground cumin**
> **1 teaspoon garam masala**
> **1 teaspoon ground mixed spice**
> **1 teaspoon turmeric**
> **1 teaspoon paprika**
> **1 teaspoon sea salt**
> **2 tablespoons peanut oil**
> **2 tablespoons sesame oil**
> **1 tablespoon white vinegar**

method

1. To make marinade, place onion, pink peppercorns, green peppercorns, coriander, black pepper, cumin, garam masala, mixed spice, turmeric, paprika, salt, peanut oil, sesame oil and vinegar into a food processor or blender and process to make a paste.
2. Rub marinade over pork, place in a glass or ceramic dish, cover and marinate in the refrigerator overnight.
3. Preheat a covered barbecue to a medium heat. Place pork on lightly oiled barbecue grill and cook, turning frequently, for 2-2 1/2 hours or until pork is tender and cooked through. Stand for 10 minutes before carving and serving.

....

Serves 8

tip from the chef
When scoring the rind take care not to cut through into the flesh.

sweet
rosemary cutlets

a

■□□ I Cooking time: 10 minutes - Preparation time: 20 minutes

method

1. Make 2 slits in the thin outer covering of each cutlet and insert a rosemary sprig into each one (a). Place prepared cutlets in a shallow dish.
2. To make marinade, place wine, honey, mustard and black pepper to taste in a bowl and mix to combine (b). Pour marinade over cutlets (c), turn to coat and marinate for 40 minutes.
3. Preheat barbecue to a high heat. Drain cutlets, place on oiled barbecue grill and cook for 4-5 minutes each side (d) or until cooked to your liking.

Serves 6

ingredients

> 12 small double lamb cutlets (allow 2 double cutlets per serve)
> 24 small sprigs rosemary

honey and wine marinade

> 1 cup/250 ml/8 fl oz red wine
> ¹/₃ cup/90 ml/3 fl oz honey
> 2 tablespoons wholegrain mustard
> crushed black peppercorns

tip from the chef

Remember always to check the barbecue area before lighting the barbecue. Do not have the barbecue too close to the house, and sweep up any dry leaves or anything that might catch fire if hit by a spark.

b

c

d

tandoori cutlets

■□□ | Cooking time: 10 minutes - Preparation time: 10 minutes

ingredients
> **2 tablespoons tandoori curry paste**
> **1 tablespoon lime juice**
> **1 tablespoon chopped fresh coriander**
> **1 teaspoon ground cumin**
> **1 teaspoon ground coriander**
> **1 teaspoon ground turmeric**
> **1 teaspoon ground cloves**
> **1¹/4 cups/250 g/8 oz natural yogurt**
> **12 lamb cutlets, trimmed of all visible fat**

yogurt mint sauce
> **¹/2 cup/100 g/3¹/2 oz natural yogurt**
> **1 clove garlic, crushed**
> **1 teaspoon ground cumin**
> **1 tablespoon finely chopped mint**

method
1. Place curry paste, lime juice, fresh coriander, cumin, ground coriander, turmeric, cloves and yogurt in a bowl and mix to combine. Place cutlets in a shallow glass or ceramic dish, spoon over yogurt mixture and turn to coat. Cover and marinate in the refrigerator overnight.
2. Drain cutlets and reserve marinade. Cook cutlets on a lightly oiled preheated hot barbecue, brushing frequently with reserved marinade, for 5 minutes each side or until tender.
3. To make sauce, place yogurt, garlic, cumin and mint in a bowl and mix to combine. Serve with cutlets.

....
Serves 6

tip from the chef
Accompany these spicy lamb cutlets with a tomato sambal. To make sambal, place 2 finely chopped tomatoes, 1 seeded and finely sliced fresh green chili, 1 tablespoon lemon juice, 1 tablespoon finely chopped onion and 1 tablespoon desiccated coconut in a bowl and mix to combine.

fresh herb chops

■☐☐ I Cooking time: 10 minutes - Preparation time: 10 minutes

method

1. To make marinade, place rosemary, thyme, garlic, oil, vinegar and lime juice in a shallow glass or ceramic dish and mix to combine. Add lamb, turn to coat, cover and marinate at room temperature for 1 hour.
2. Preheat barbecue to a high heat. Drain lamb, place on lightly oiled barbecue and cook for 3-5 minutes each side or until chops are cooked to your liking.

....
Serves 6

ingredients

> **12 lamb neck chops, trimmed of excess fat**

fresh herb marinade

> **2 tablespoons chopped fresh rosemary**
> **2 tablespoons chopped fresh thyme**
> **2 cloves garlic, crushed**
> **1/4 cup/60 ml/2 fl oz olive oil**
> **1/4 cup/60 ml/2 fl oz balsamic or red wine vinegar**
> **2 tablespoons lime juice**

tip from the chef

Long-handled tongs are a must for turning food without burning your hands.

barbecued
port-glazed lamb

■□□ I Cooking time: 2 hours - Preparation time: 10 minutes

ingredients

> **2.5 kg/5 lb leg of lamb**
> **1 cup/250 ml/8 fl oz port**
> **1 1/2 cups/375 ml/12 fl oz water**

port glaze

> **4 tablespoons Dijon mustard**
> **2 teaspoons finely grated orange rind**
> **1/2 teaspoon grated nutmeg**
> **1 1/2 cups/375 ml/12 fl oz port**
> **1/2 cup/125 ml/4 fl oz honey**
> **2 tablespoons balsamic vinegar**

method

1. Preheat covered barbecue to a medium heat.
2. To make glaze, place mustard, orange rind, nutmeg, port, honey and vinegar in a saucepan, bring to simmering over a low heat and simmer until mixture thickens and reduces slightly.
3. Place lamb on a wire rack set in a roasting tin and brush with glaze. Pour port and water into roasting tin, place on barbecue, cover with lid and cook for 2 hours, brushing with glaze at 15-minute intervals, or until cooked to your liking.

....

Serves 8

tip from the chef
Check the quantity of liquid in the roasting tin regularly during cooking and add more water if required.

grilled
apple stacks

a

■□□ I Cooking time: 5 minutes - Preparation time: 10 minutes

method

1. Preheat barbecue to a low heat. Cut each apple crosswise into 4 thick slices (a). Combine lemon juice and honey and brush over apple slices (b).
2. Cook apple slices on oiled barbecue grill (c) for 2 minutes each side or until golden. Transfer apples to a bowl and chill.
3. To make filling, place ricotta cheese, sugar, lemon juice and vanilla essence in a food processor or blender and process until smooth (d).
4. To serve, place an apple slice on each serving plate. Top with a spoonful of ricotta filling and another apple slice.

....
Serves 6

ingredients

> **3 apples, cored**
> **2 tablespoons lemon juice**
> **1 tablespoon honey**

ricotta filling

> **250 g/8 oz ricotta cheese**
> **2 tablespoons sugar**
> **2 tablespoons lemon juice**
> **1 teaspoon vanilla essence**

tip from the chef

For this recipe, purchase fresh ricotta cheese in a piece. It has a smoother texture than that which comes in the small tubs. Fresh ricotta cheese is available from specialty cheese shops, delicatessens and some supermarkets.

b

c

d

grilled nectarines

■□□ I Cooking time: 5 minutes - Preparation time: 10 minutes

ingredients

> 1/4 cup/60 g/2 oz caster sugar
> 1/3 cup/90 ml/3 fl oz marsala or sweet sherry
> 1 tablespoon lemon juice
> 6 nectarines, stoned and quartered

vanilla mascarpone

> 100 g/3 1/2 oz ricotta cheese
> 155 g/5 oz mascarpone
> 2 tablespoons sugar
> 1 teaspoon vanilla essence
> 1 tablespoon marsala or sweet sherry

method

1. Preheat barbecue to a medium heat. Place caster sugar, marsala or sherry and lemon juice in a bowl and mix to combine. Add nectarines (a) and macerate for 5 minutes.
2. Drain nectarines and reserve liquid. Place nectarines on barbecue plate and cook for 1 minute each side (b) or until golden. Return nectarines to macerating liquid (c) until ready to serve.
3. For mascarpone, place ricotta cheese, mascarpone, sugar, vanilla and marsala or sherry in a bowl (d) and beat until smooth. Serve with nectarines.

....
Serves 6

tip from the chef
This recipe is also delicious made with fresh peaches.

a

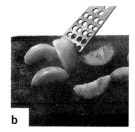

b

c

d

grilled
strawberry kebabs

■□□ | Cooking time: 1 minute - Preparation time: 5 minutes

method

1. Preheat barbecue to a high heat.
2. Thread strawberries onto lightly oiled wooden skewers. Brush strawberries with vinegar, then roll in icing sugar.
3. Cook kebabs on oiled barbecue grill for 10 seconds each side or until icing sugar caramelizes. Serve immediately with ice cream.

ingredients

> **500 g/1 lb strawberries, halved**
> **¼ cup/60 ml/2 fl oz balsamic vinegar**
> **1½ cups/220 g/7 oz icing sugar**
> **vanilla ice cream**

Serves 8

tip from the chef

Remember to soak bamboo or wooden skewers in water before using –this helps to prevent them from burning during cooking. Before threading food onto skewers, lightly oil them so that the cooked food is easy to remove. For this recipe, use a light tasting oil such as canola or sunflower.

coconut
rice parcels

■□□ I Cooking time: 30 minutes - Preparation time: 15 minutes

method

1. Preheat barbecue to a medium-high heat. Place rice, water, coconut milk and sugar in a saucepan and bring to the boil over a high heat. Reduce heat and simmer for 10-15 minutes or until liquid is absorbed.
2. Place banana leaves, if using, in a shallow dish, pour over boiling water to cover and soak for 5 minutes. Drain.
3. Divide half the rice between the banana leaves or foil. Spread rice out evenly, then top with banana mixture. Cover with remaining rice, fold banana leaf or aluminum foil to enclose and secure with a wooden toothpick or cocktail stick. Cook parcels on barbecue grill for 2 minutes each side or until heated through.

ingredients

> 375 g/12 oz jasmine rice
> 2 cups/500 ml/16 fl oz water
> 200 ml/6½ fl oz coconut milk
> ¼ cup/60 g/2 oz sugar
> 4 x 30 cm/12 in squares banana leaf or aluminum foil
> 1 banana, mashed with 1 tablespoon lemon juice

Serves 4

tip from the chef

These rice parcels are delicious served with coconut or vanilla ice cream. Banana leaves can be purchased from Oriental food shops and some greengrocers and supermarkets. Leaves are not eaten but they impart distinctive flavor to the rice. They can be softened by blanching as in this recipe. Alternatively, heat in a covered microwavable dish on High (100%) for 45-60 seconds or until soft. For easier wrapping, remove the thick mid-rib from the leaves.

index